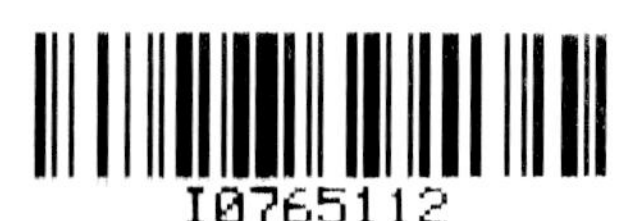

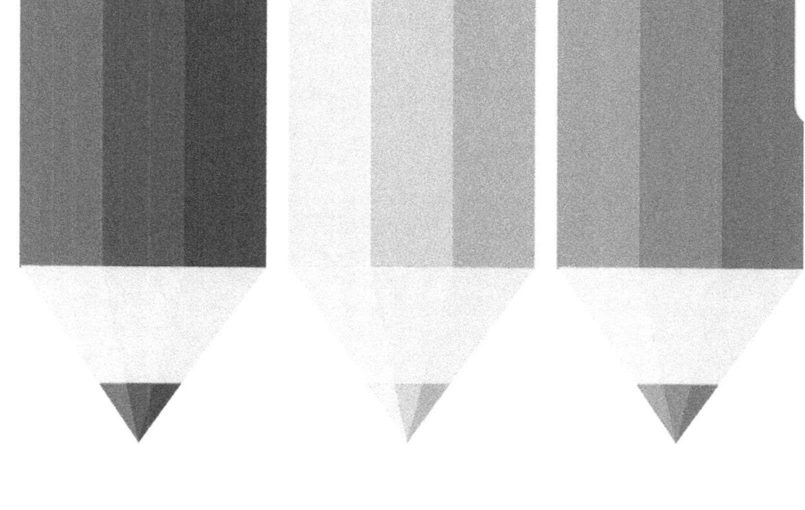

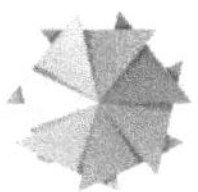 # THIS BOOK BELONG TO: 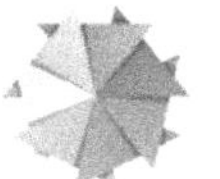

....

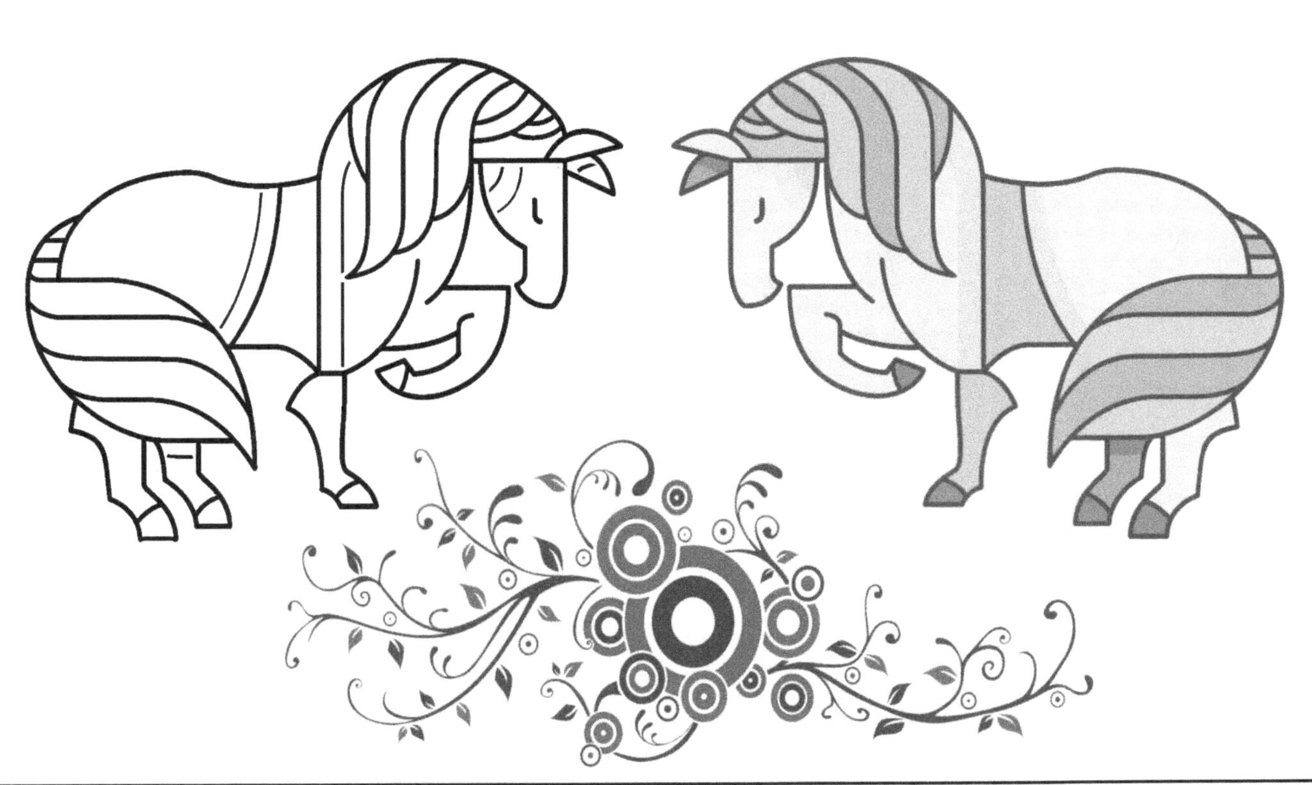

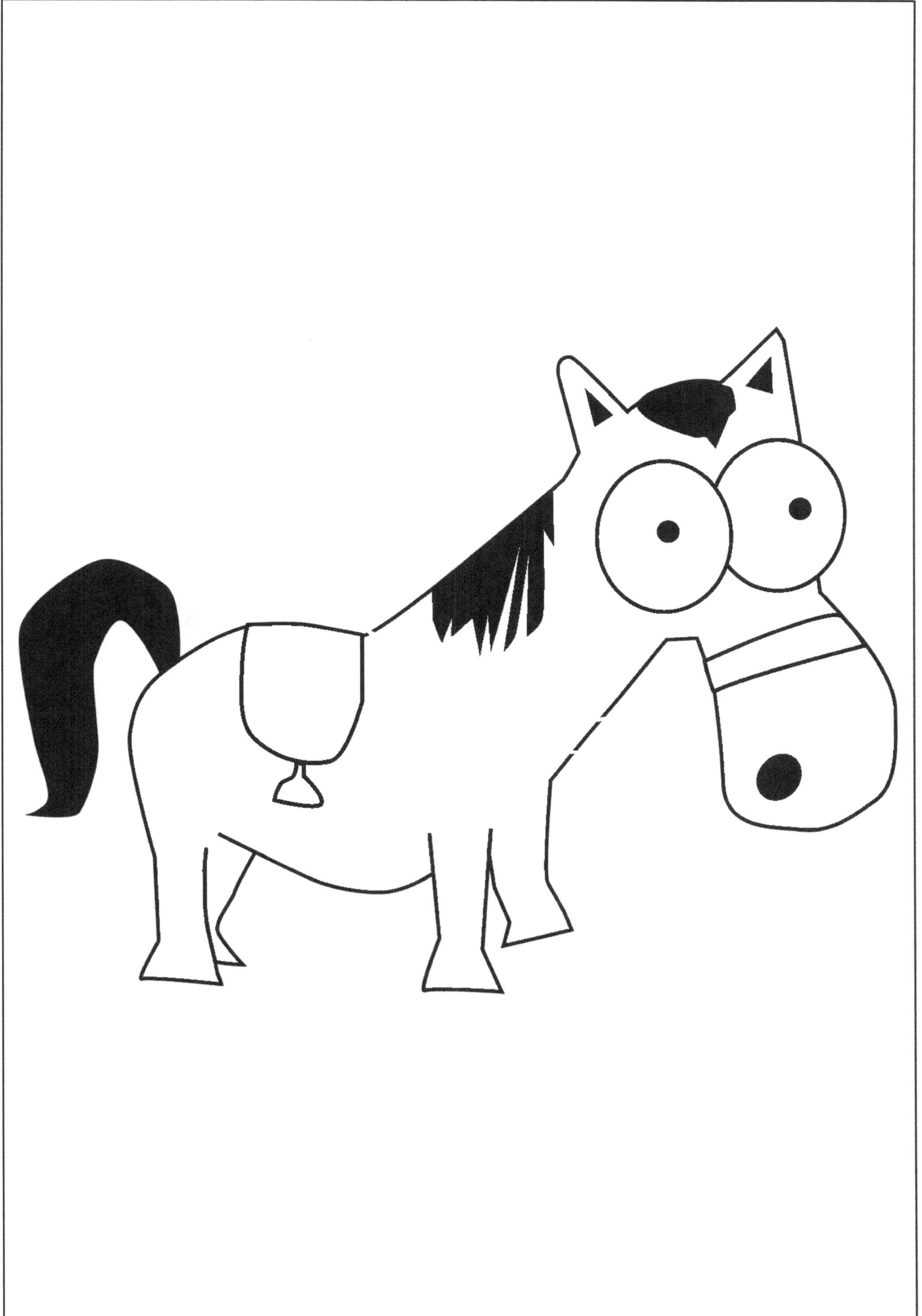

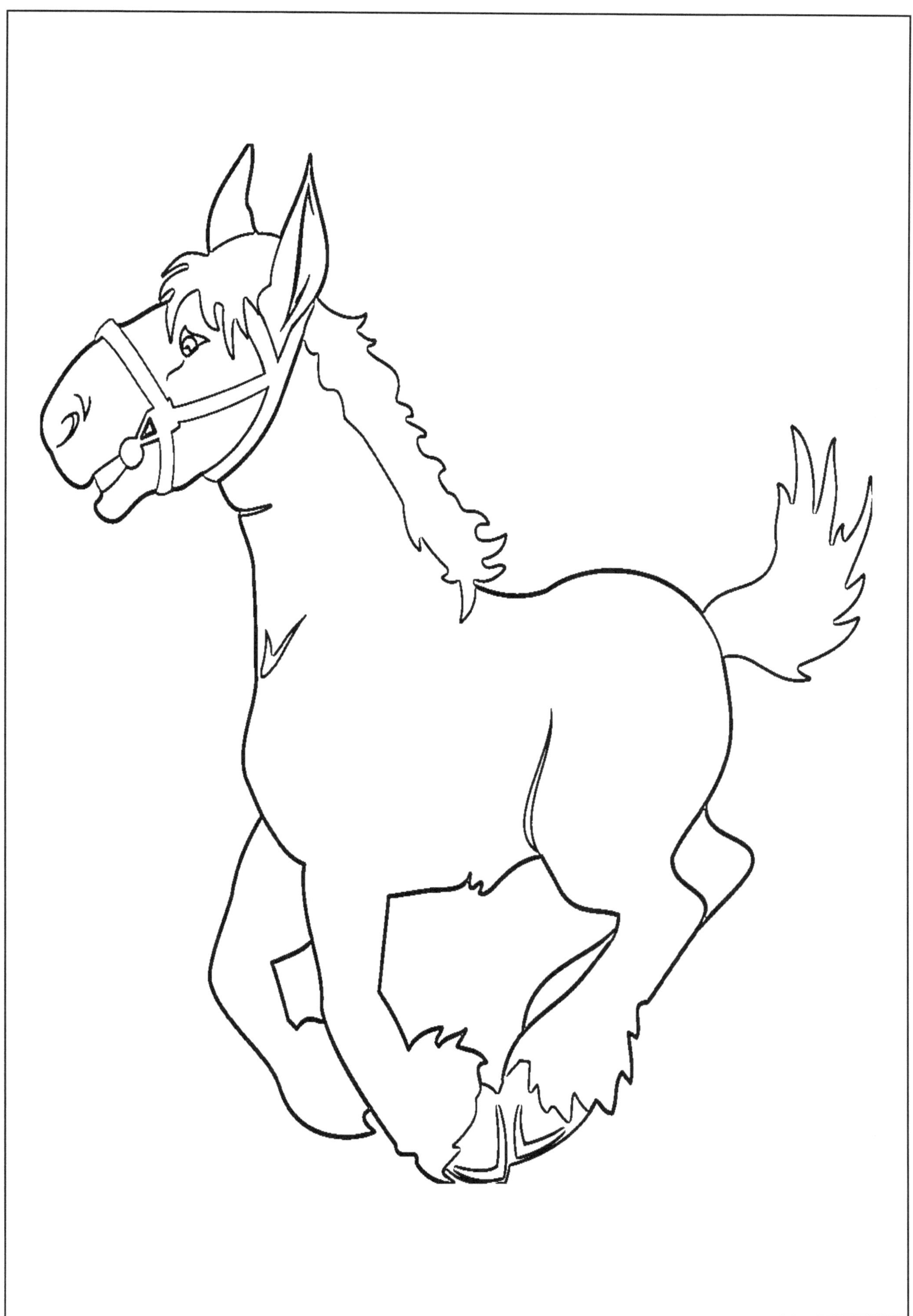

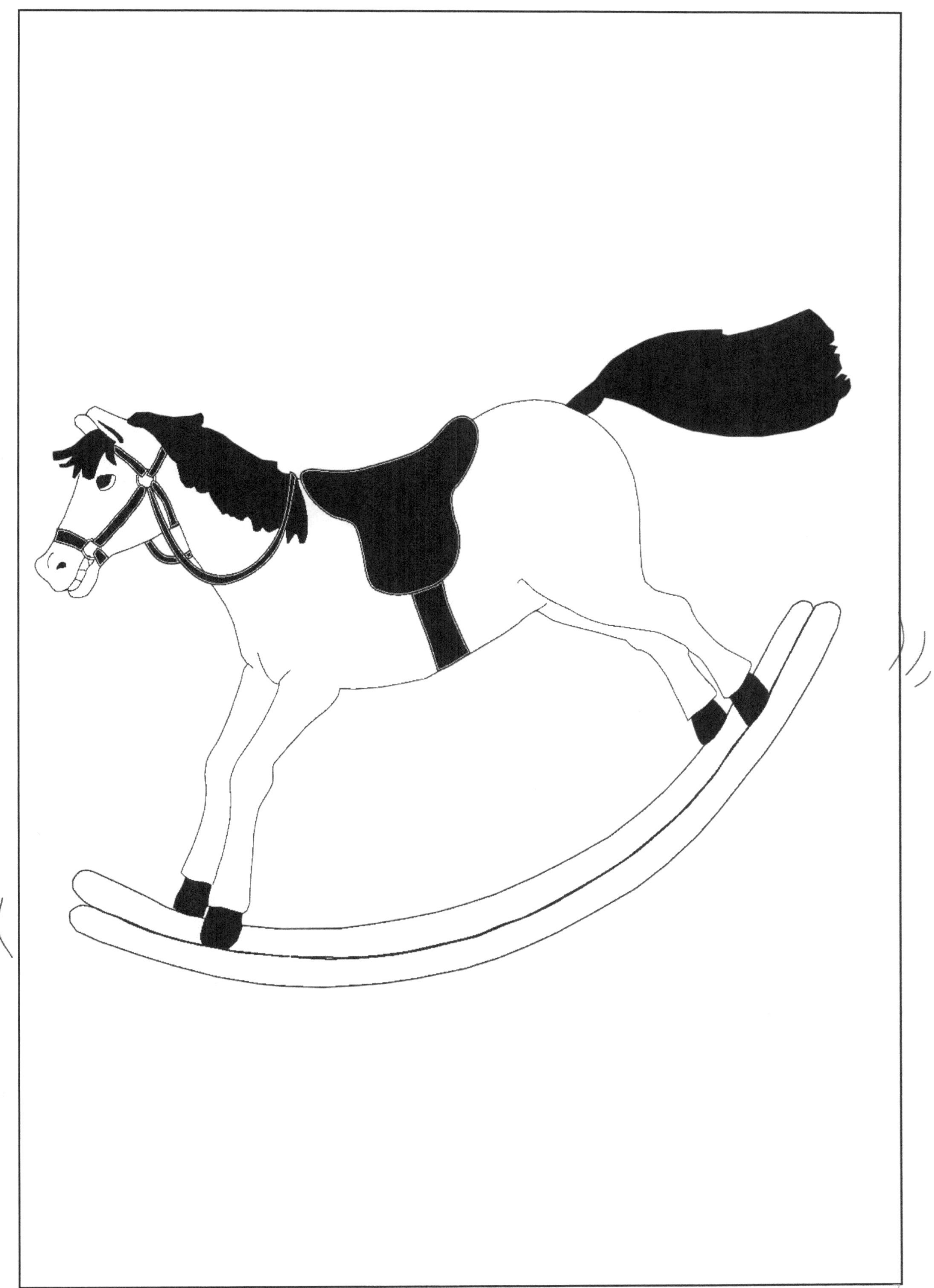

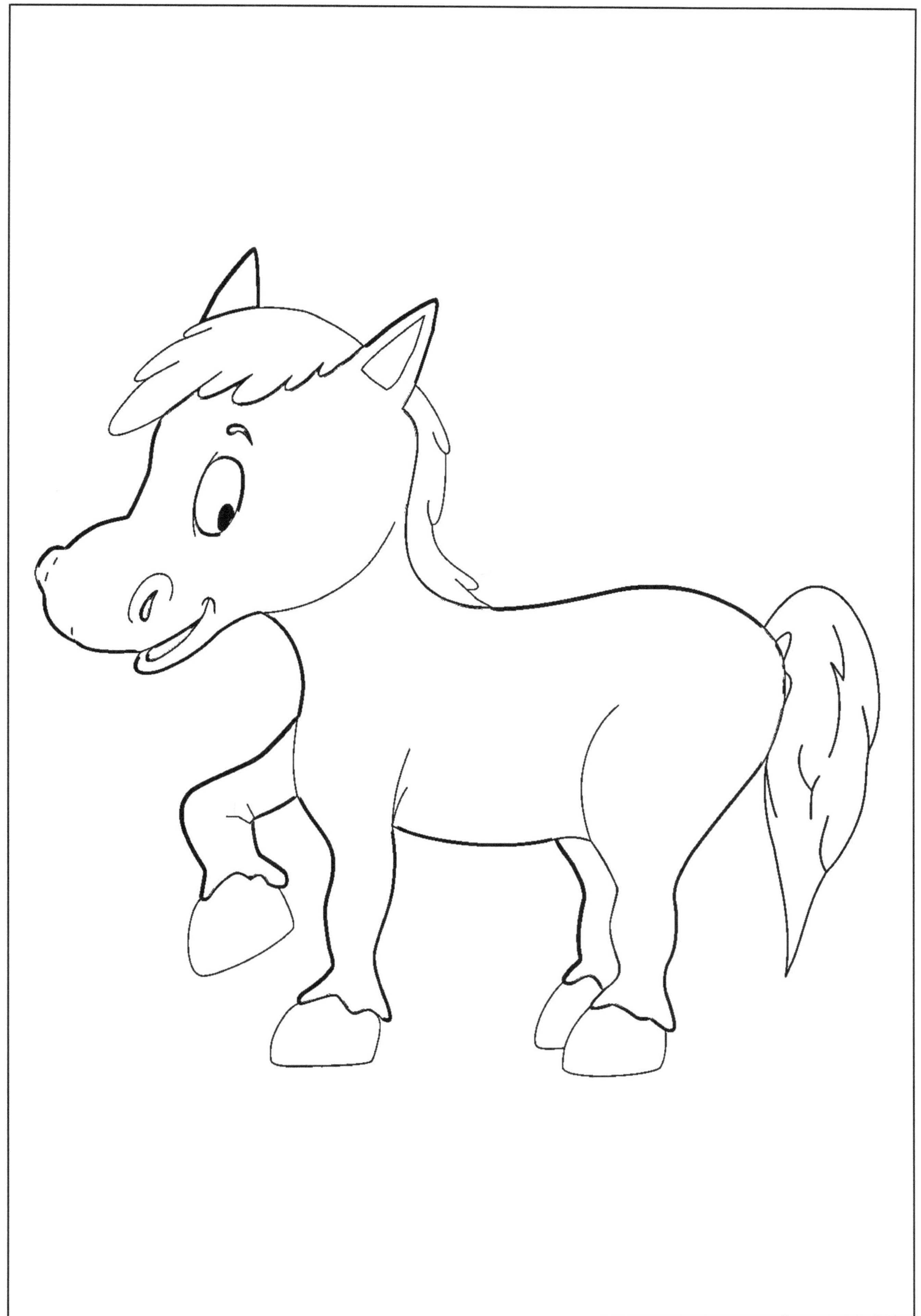

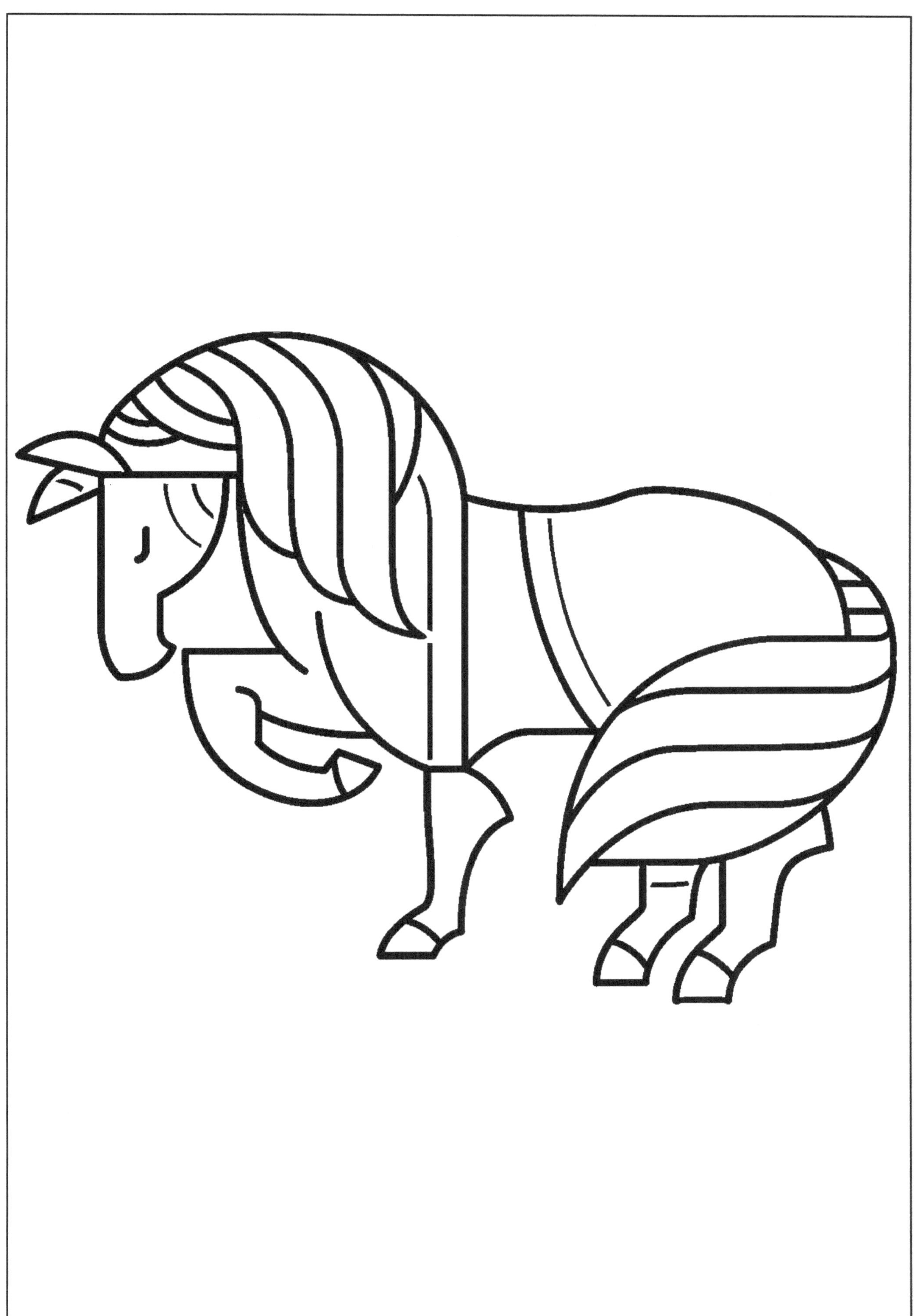

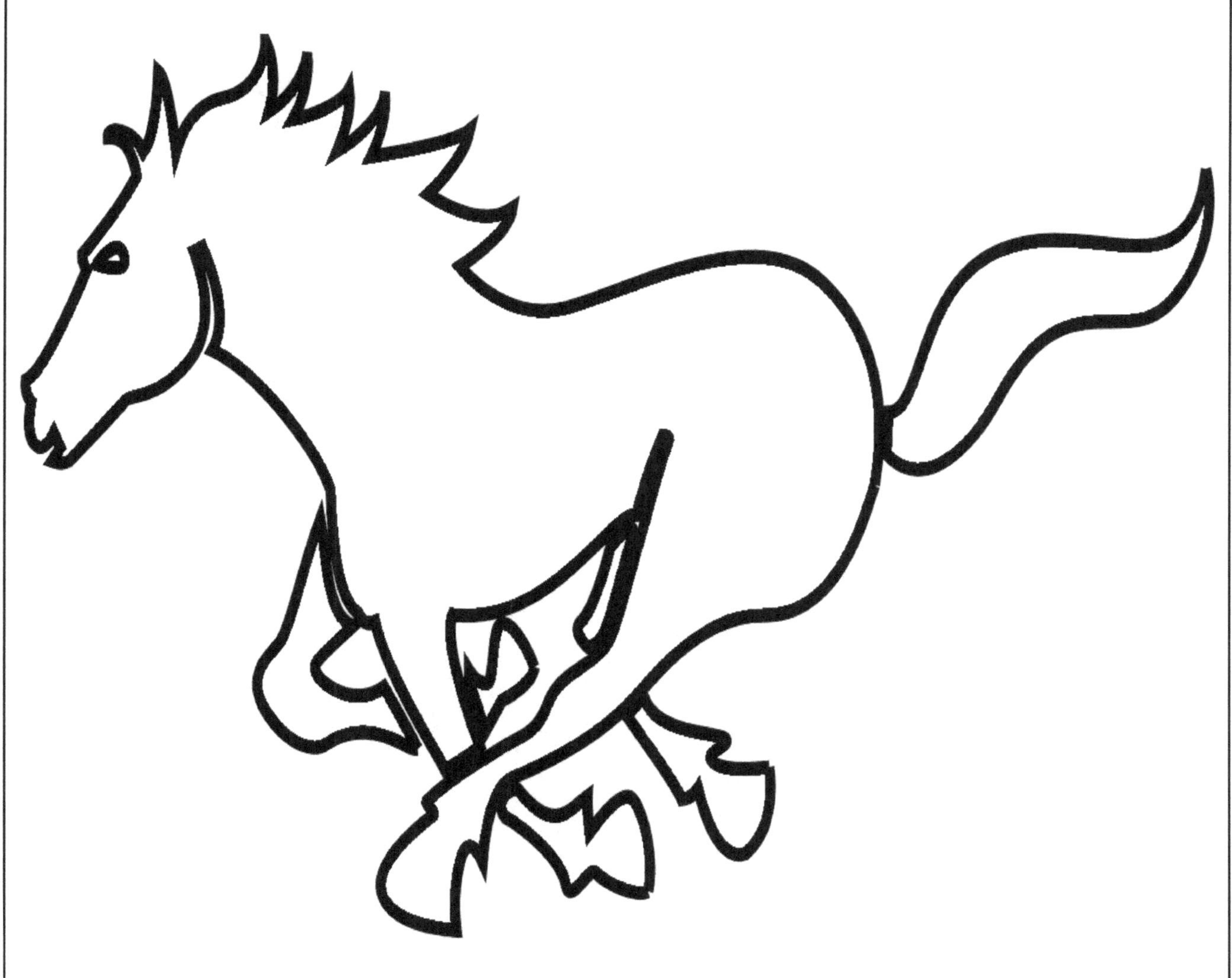

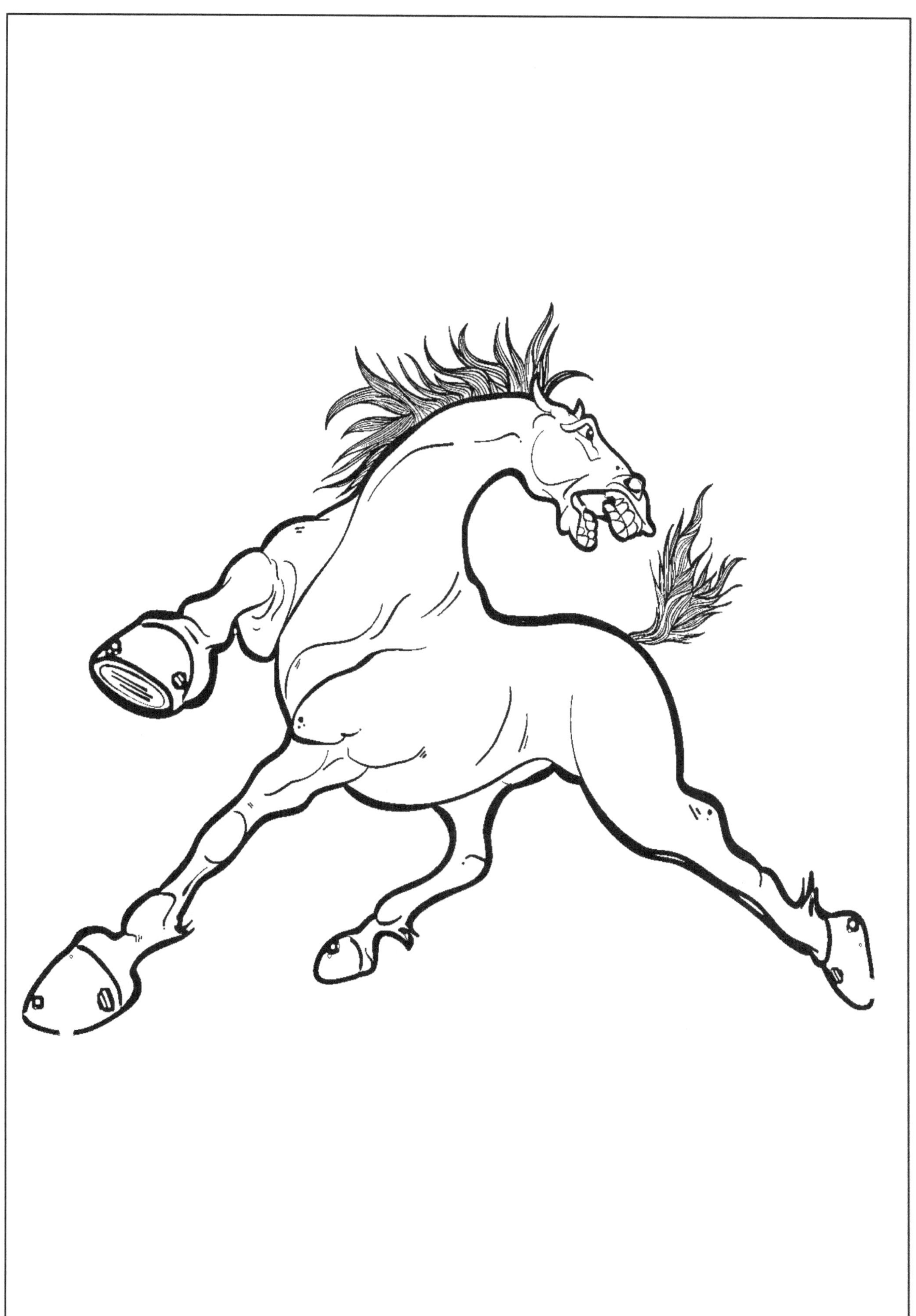

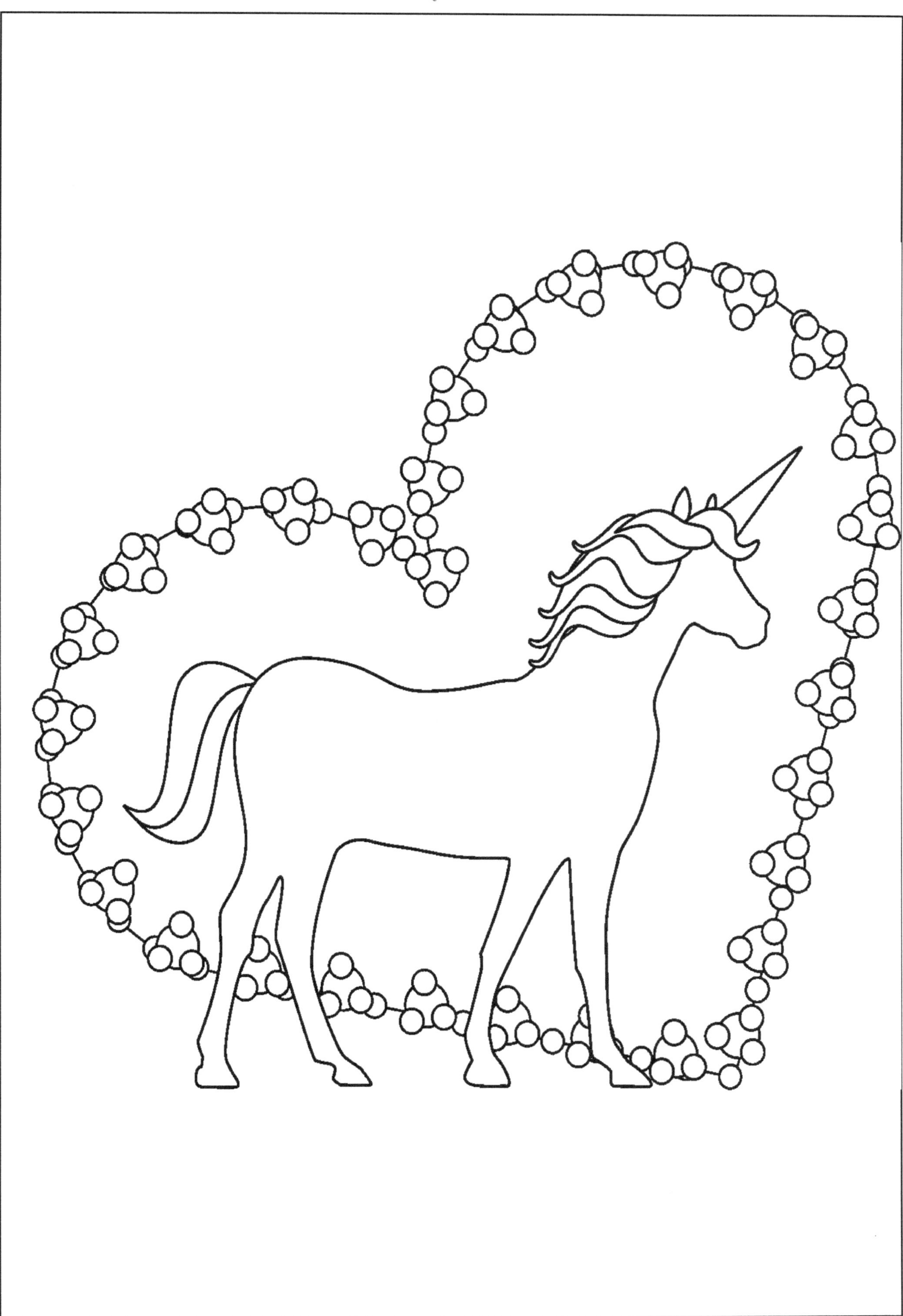

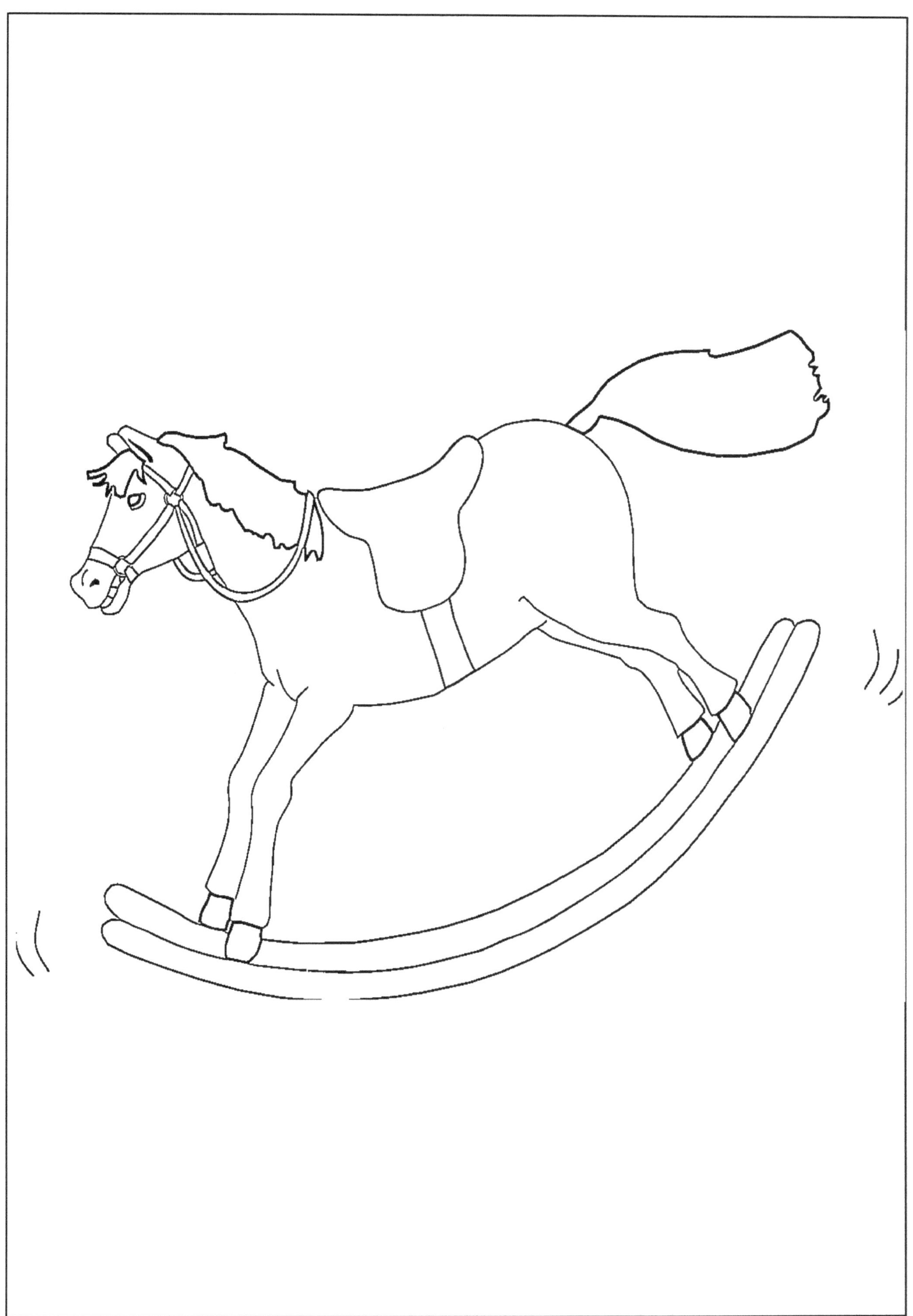

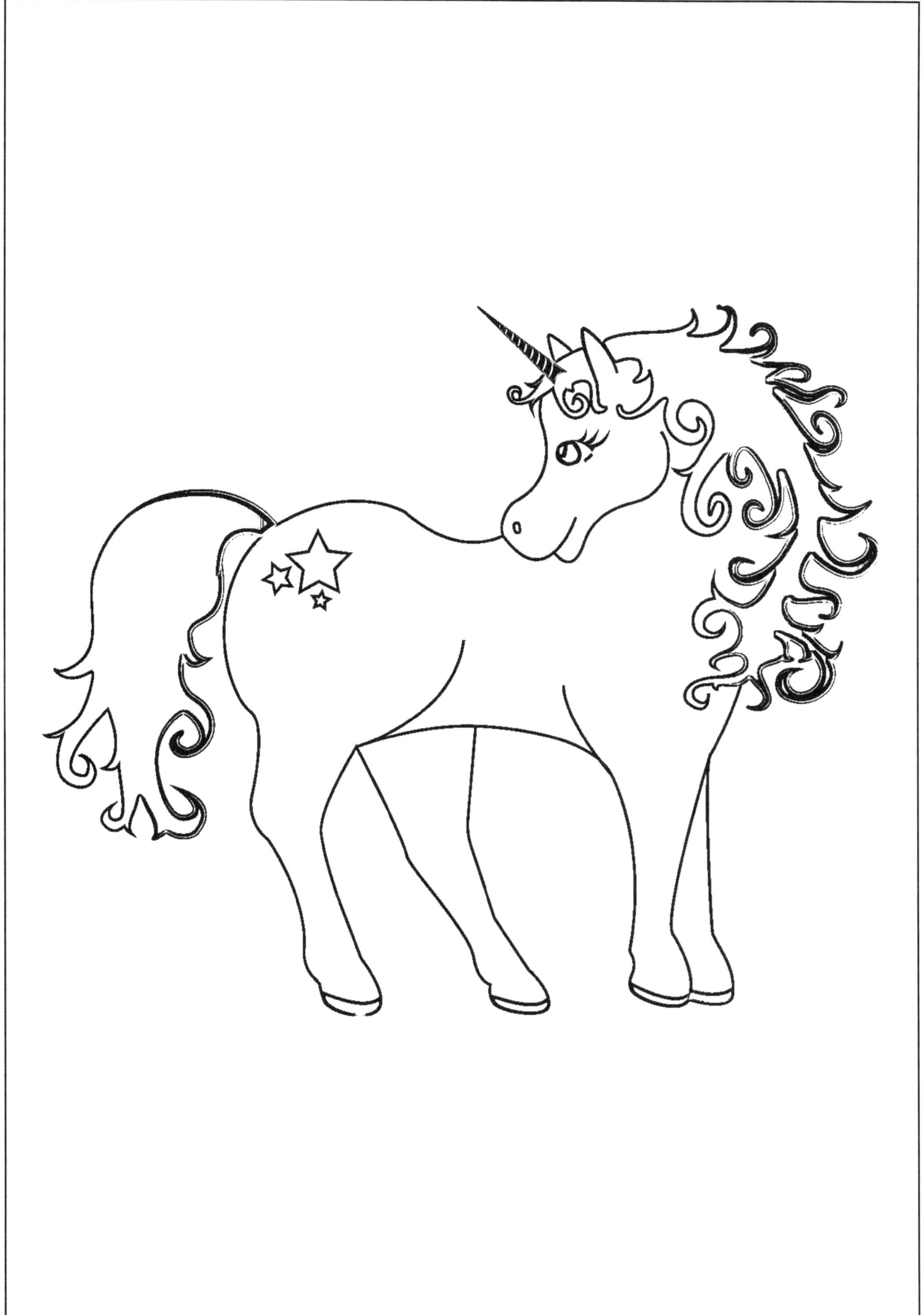

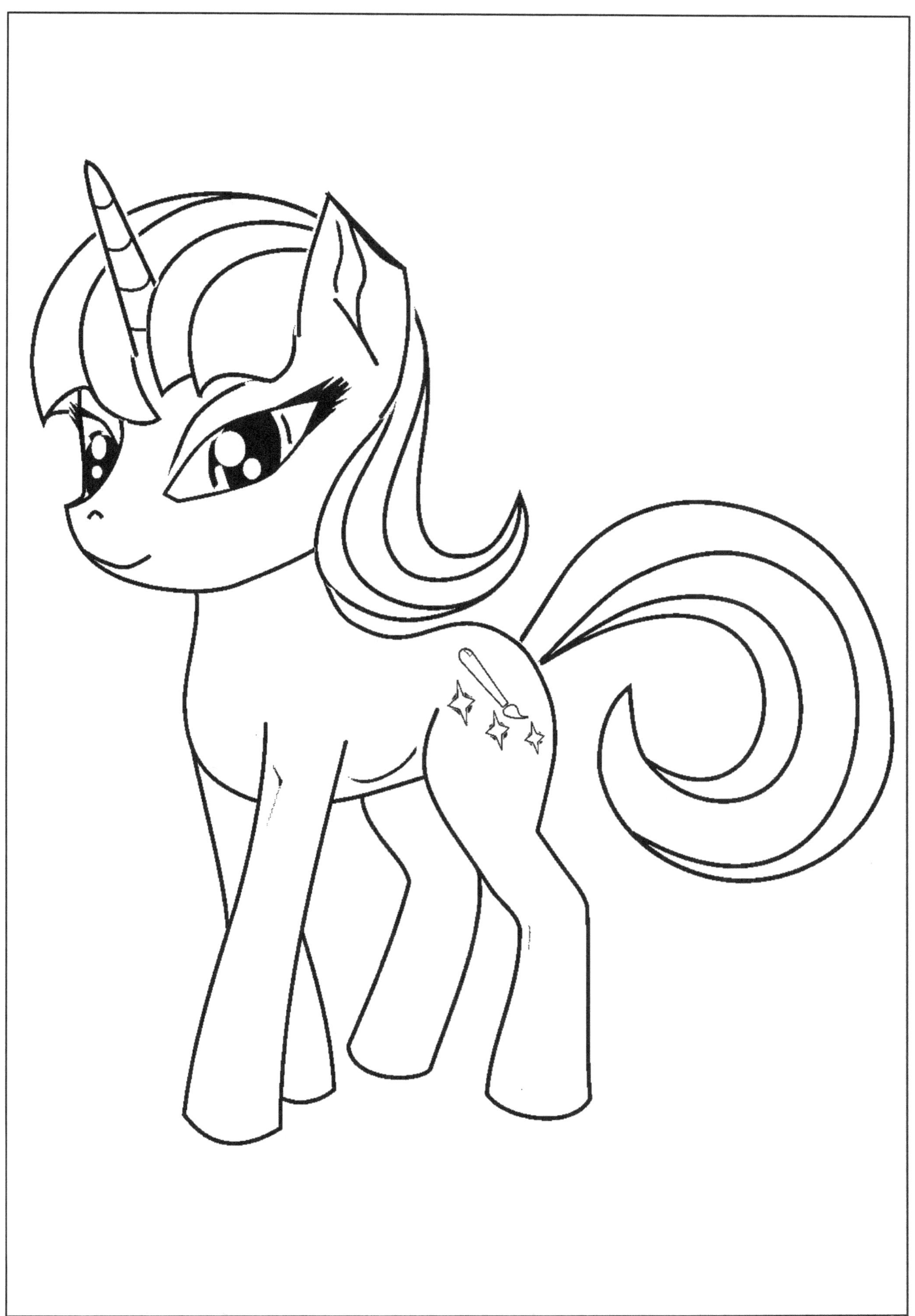

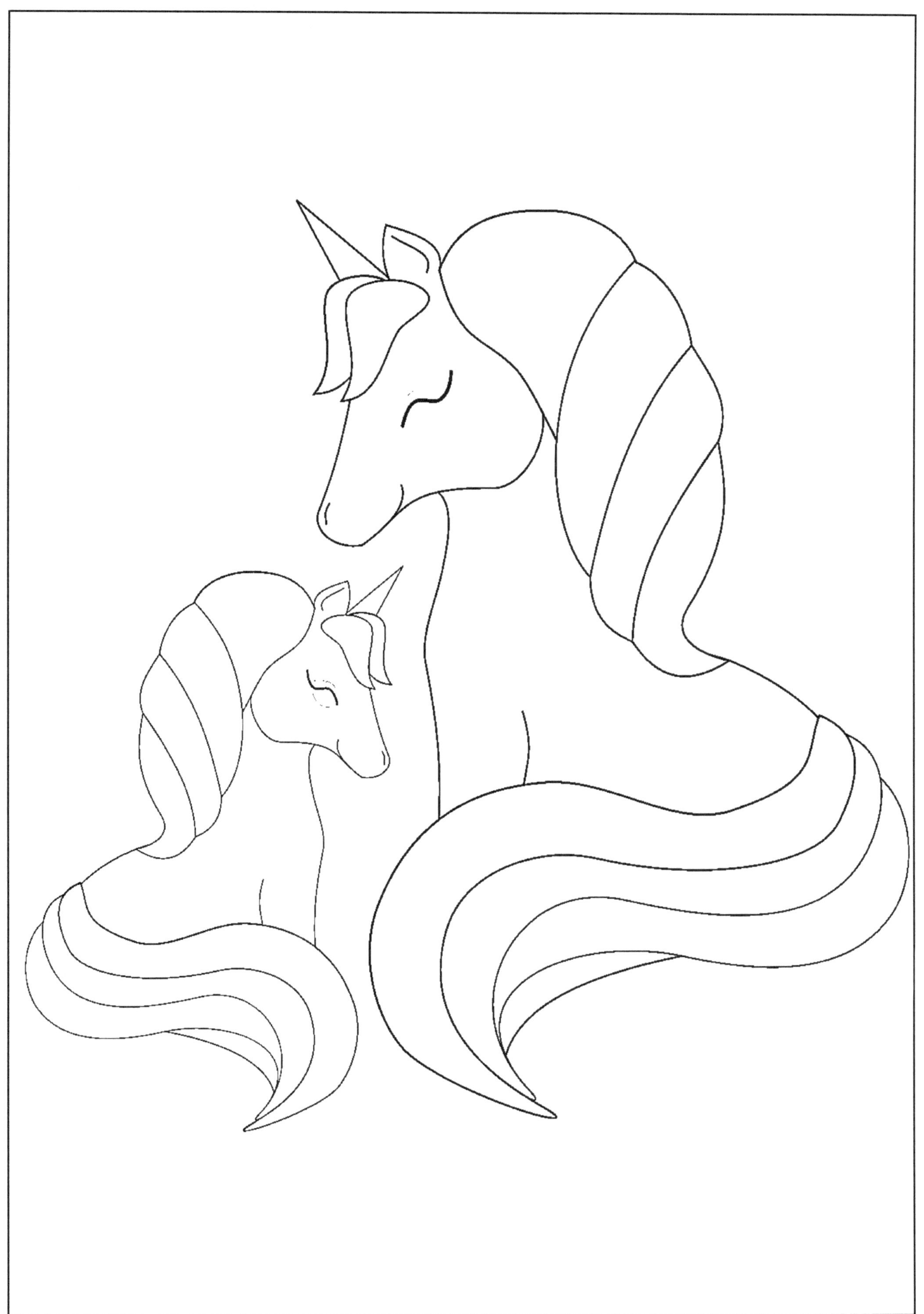

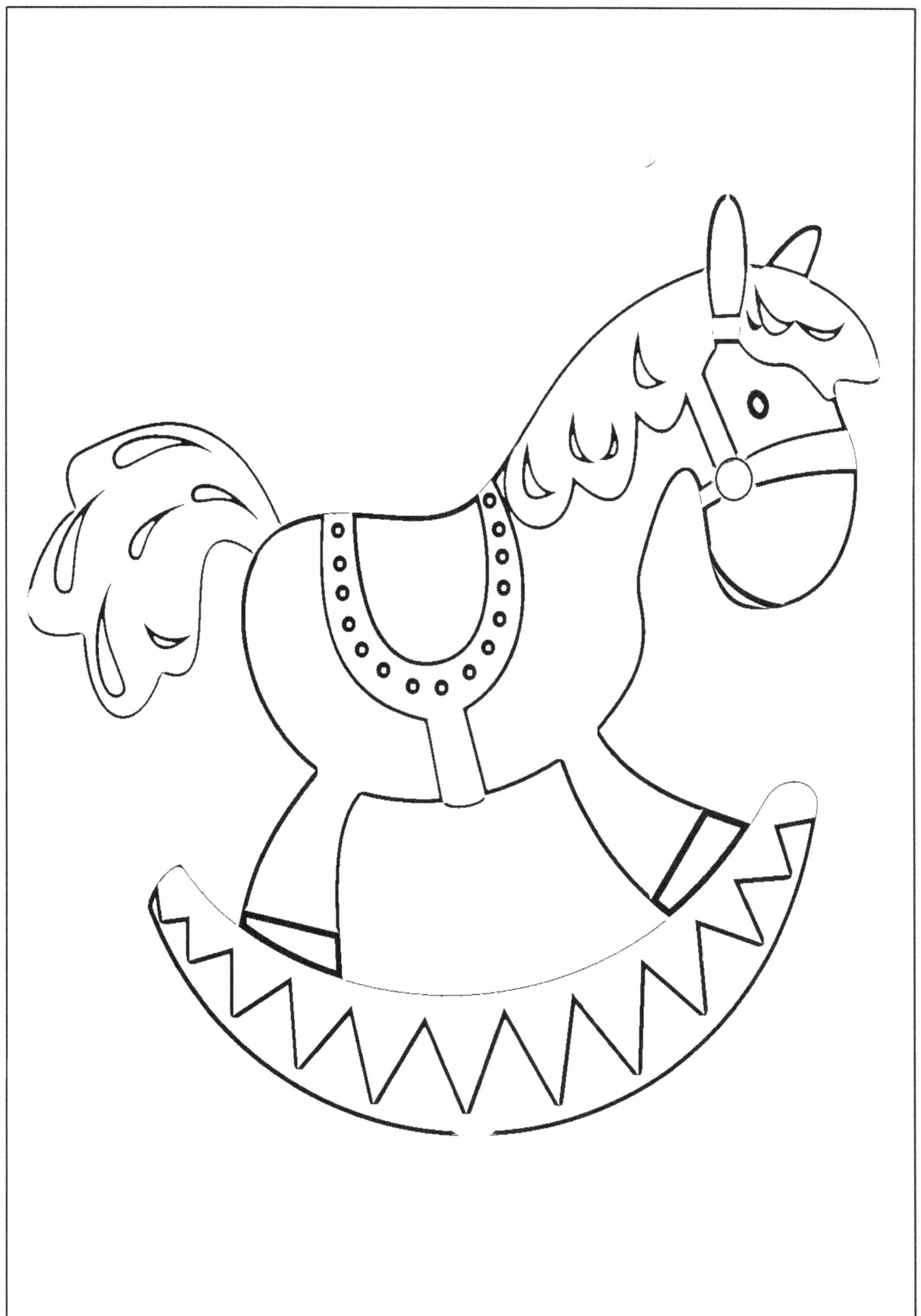

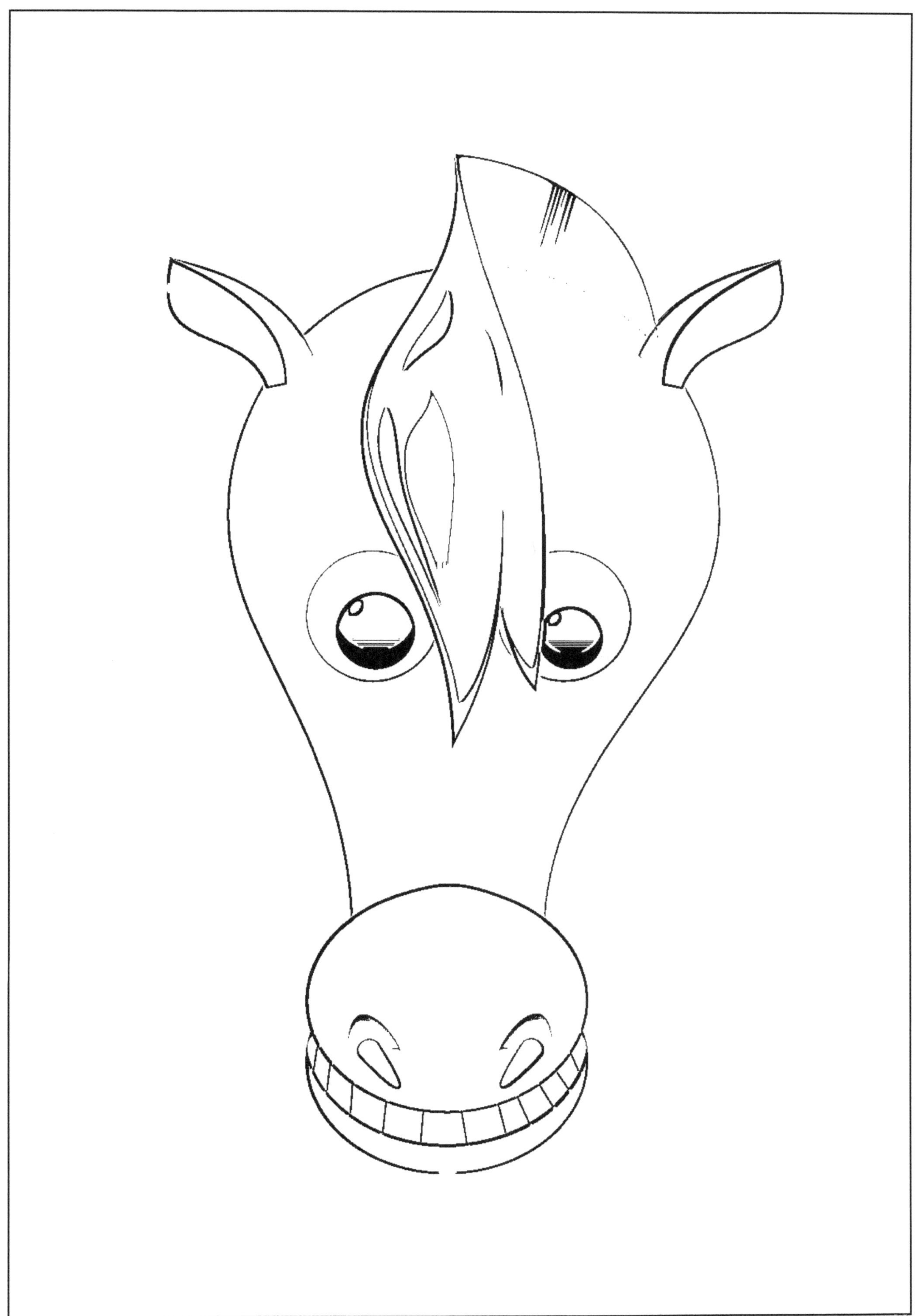

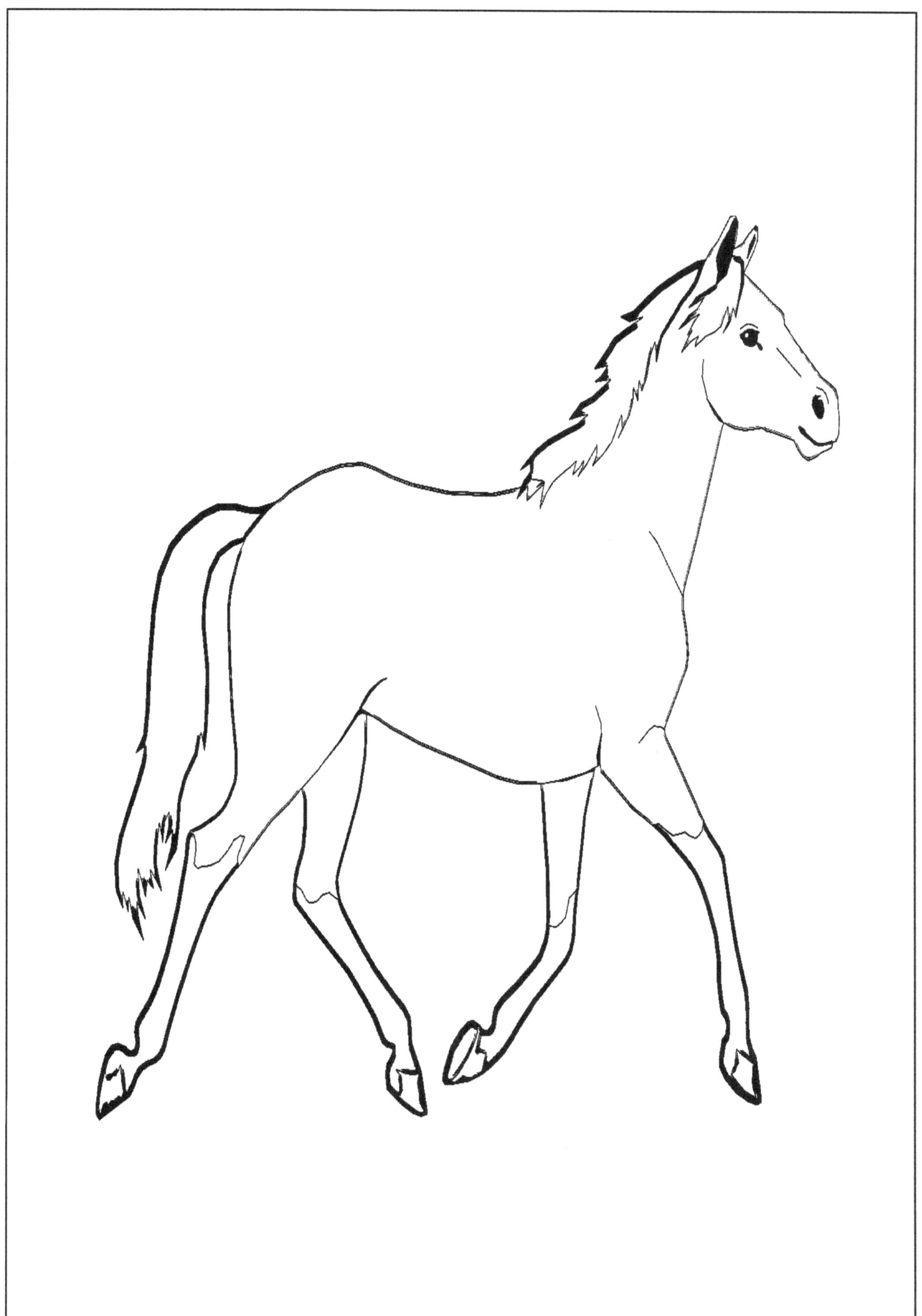

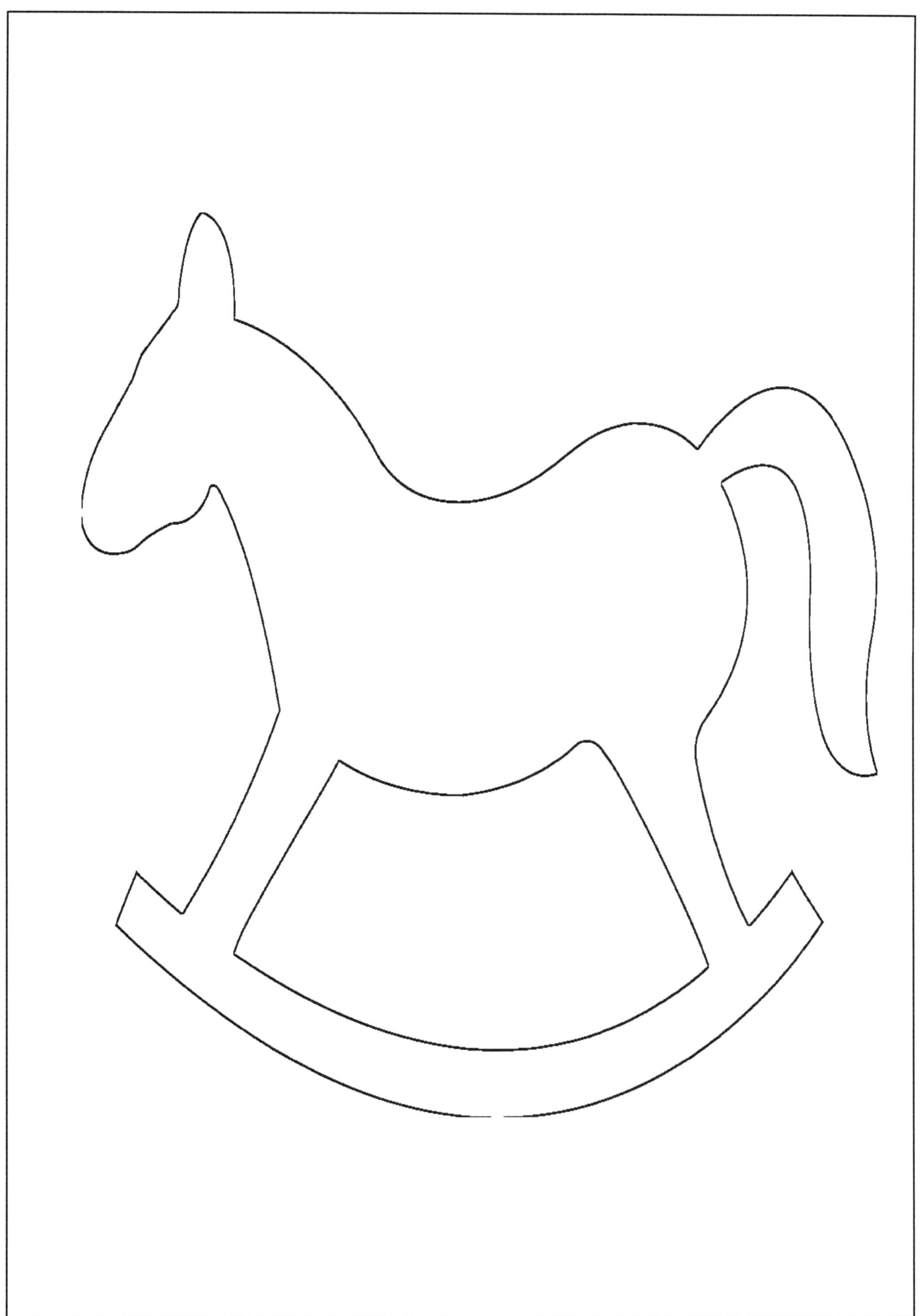

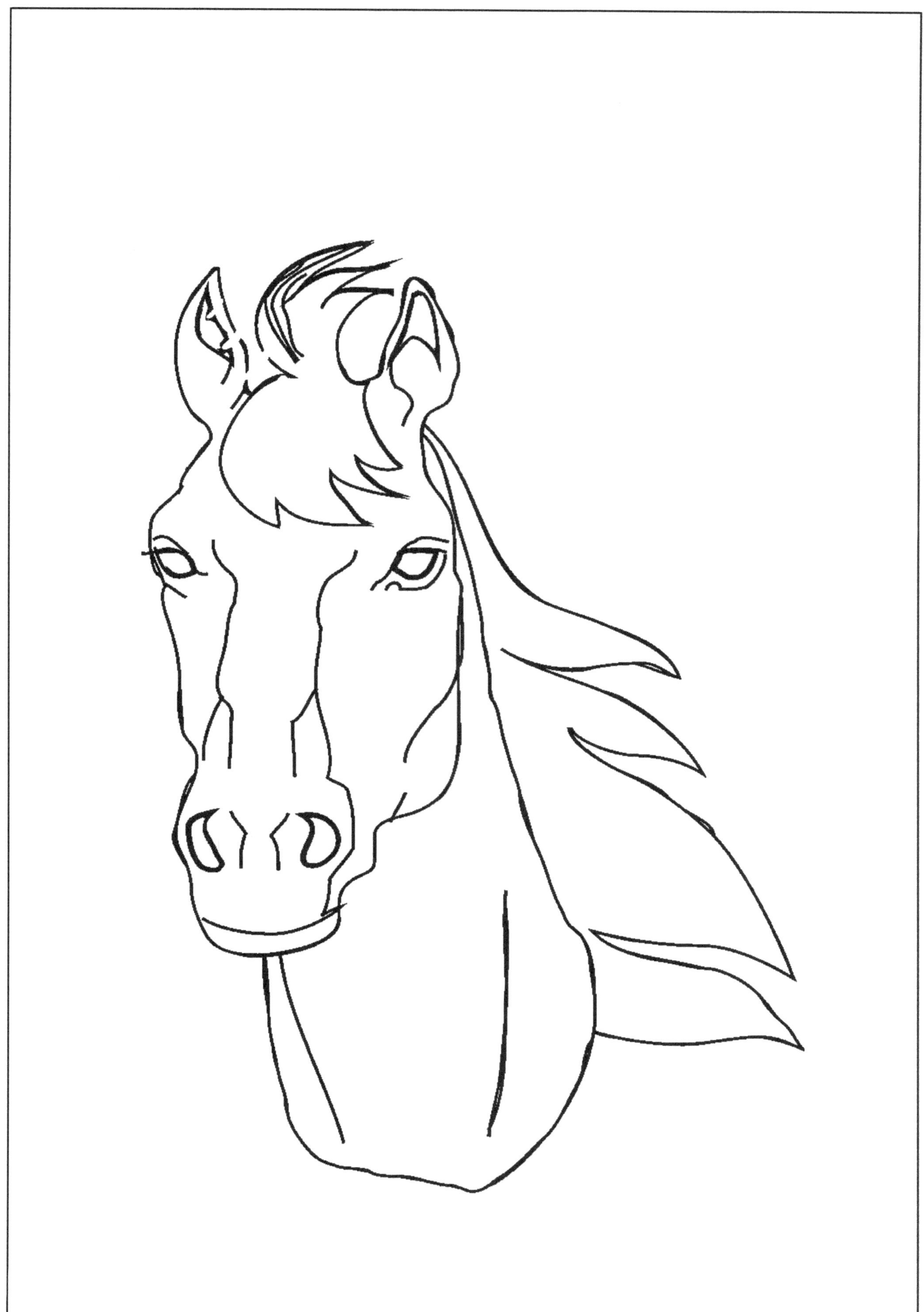

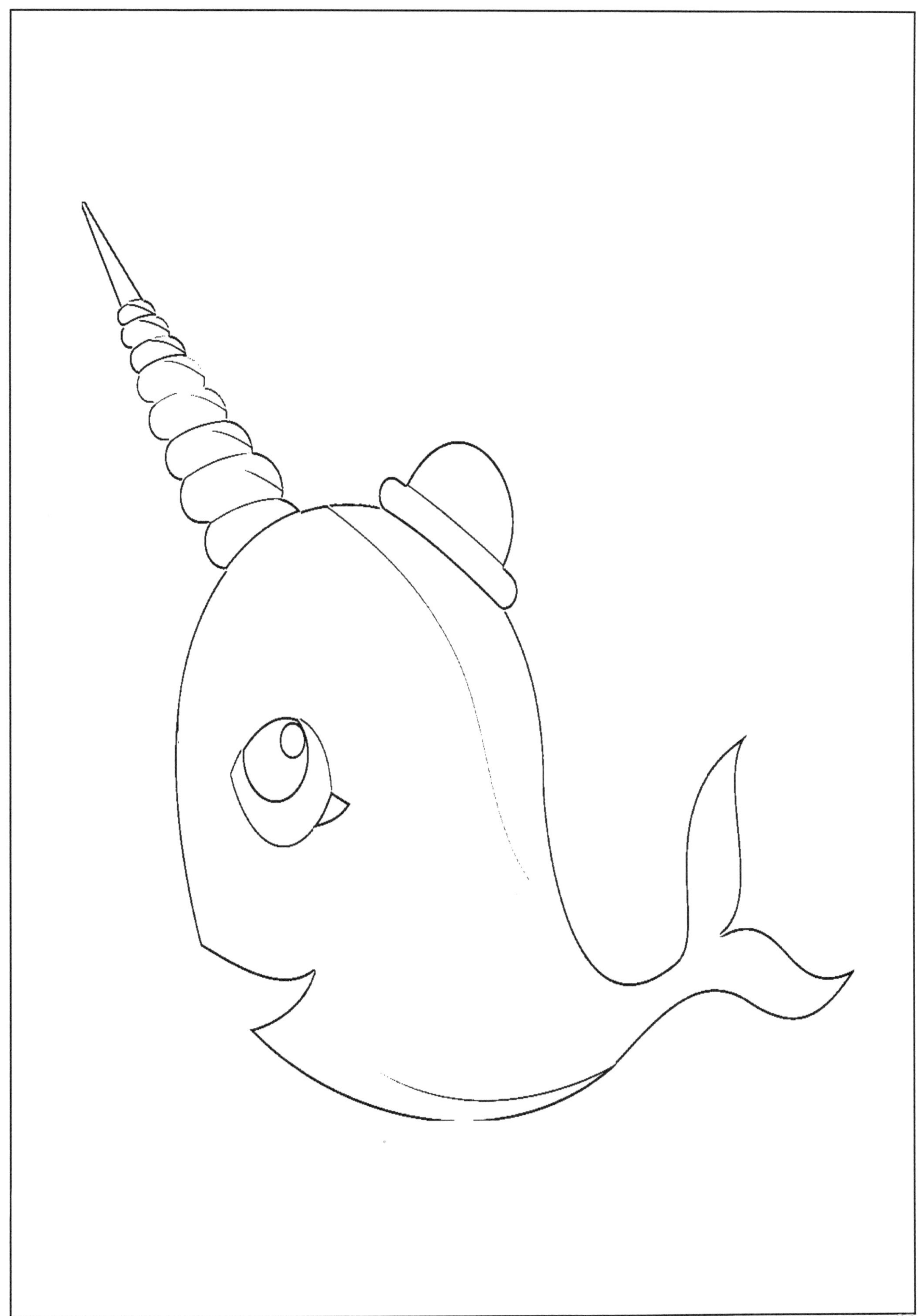

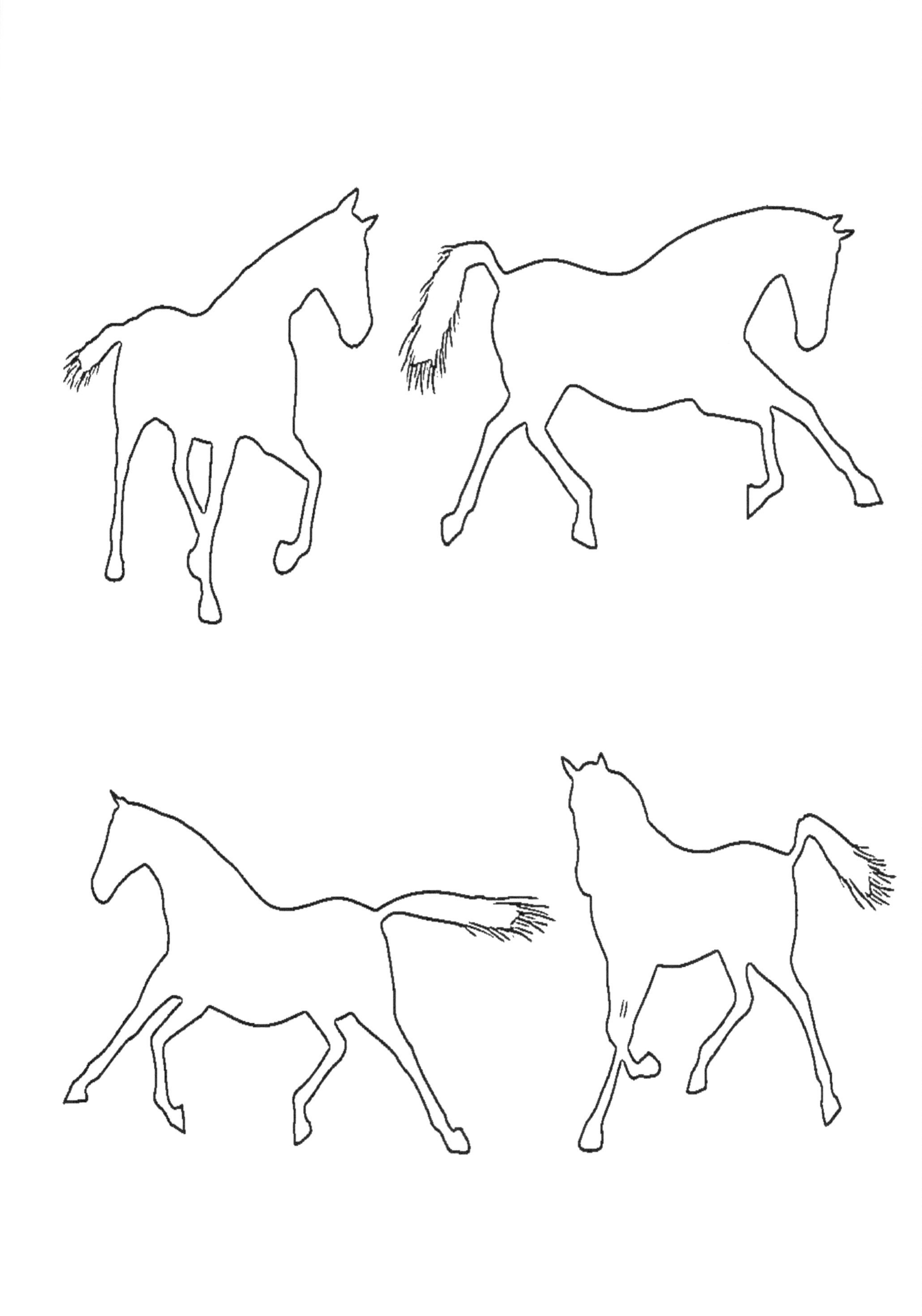

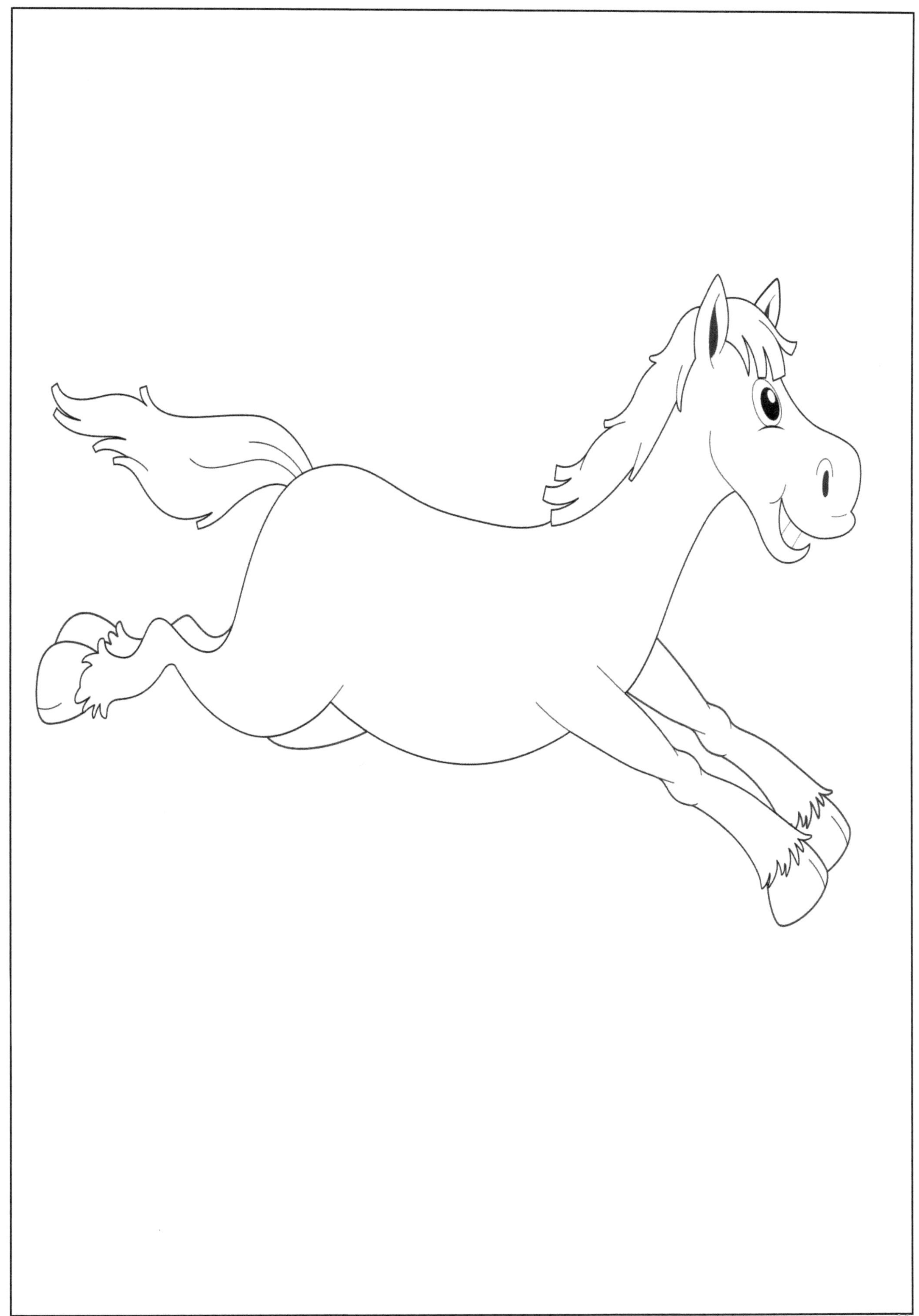

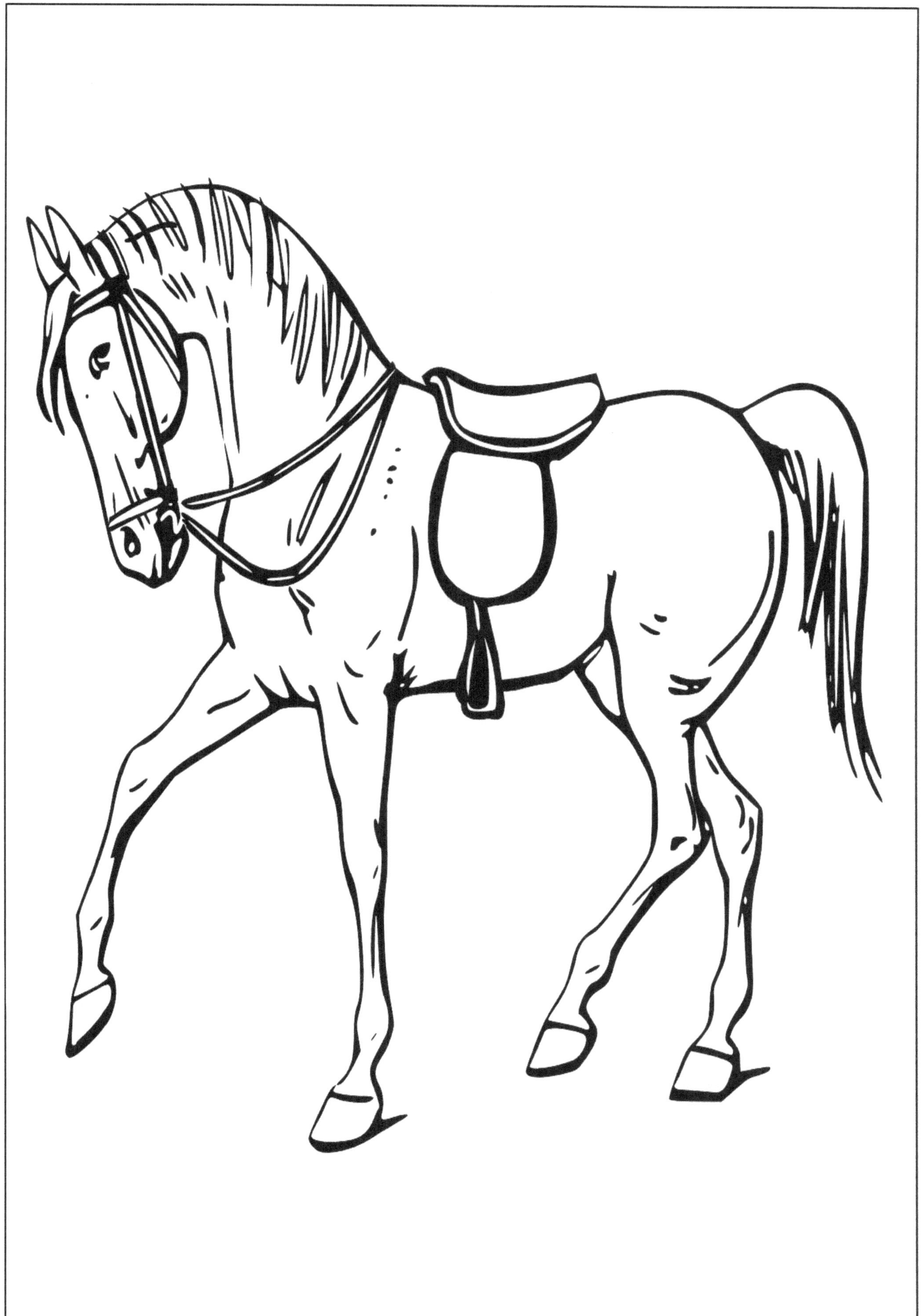

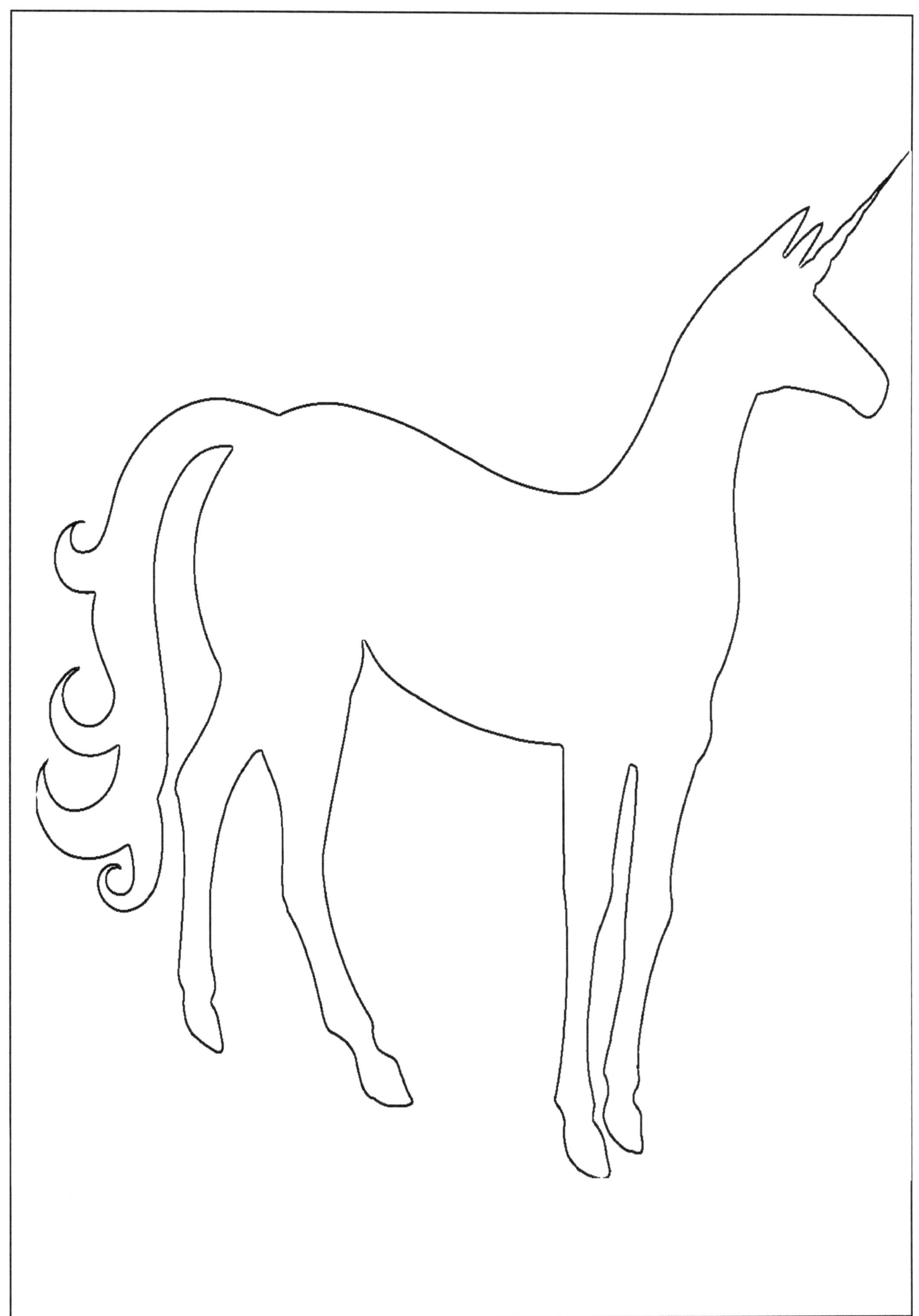

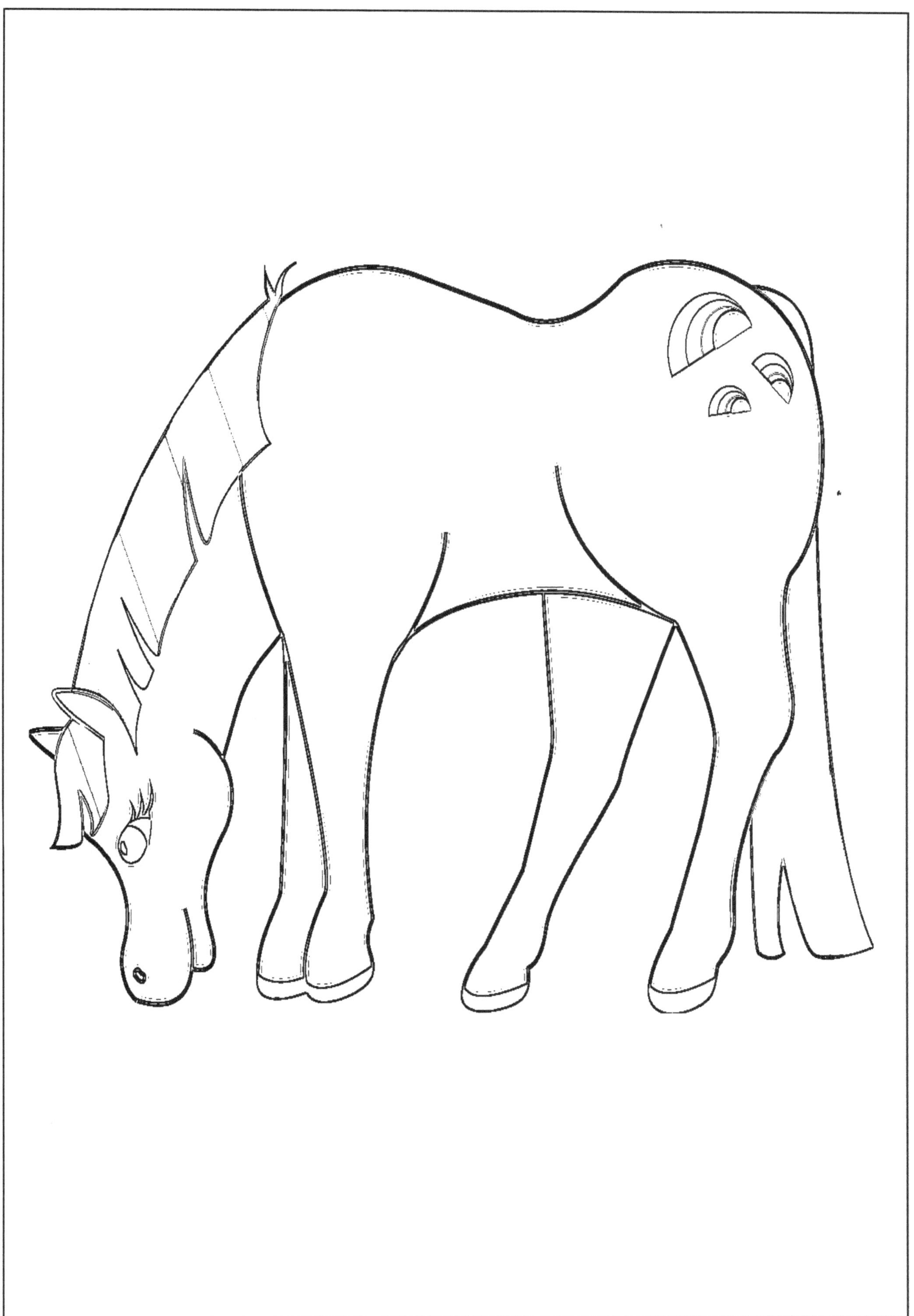

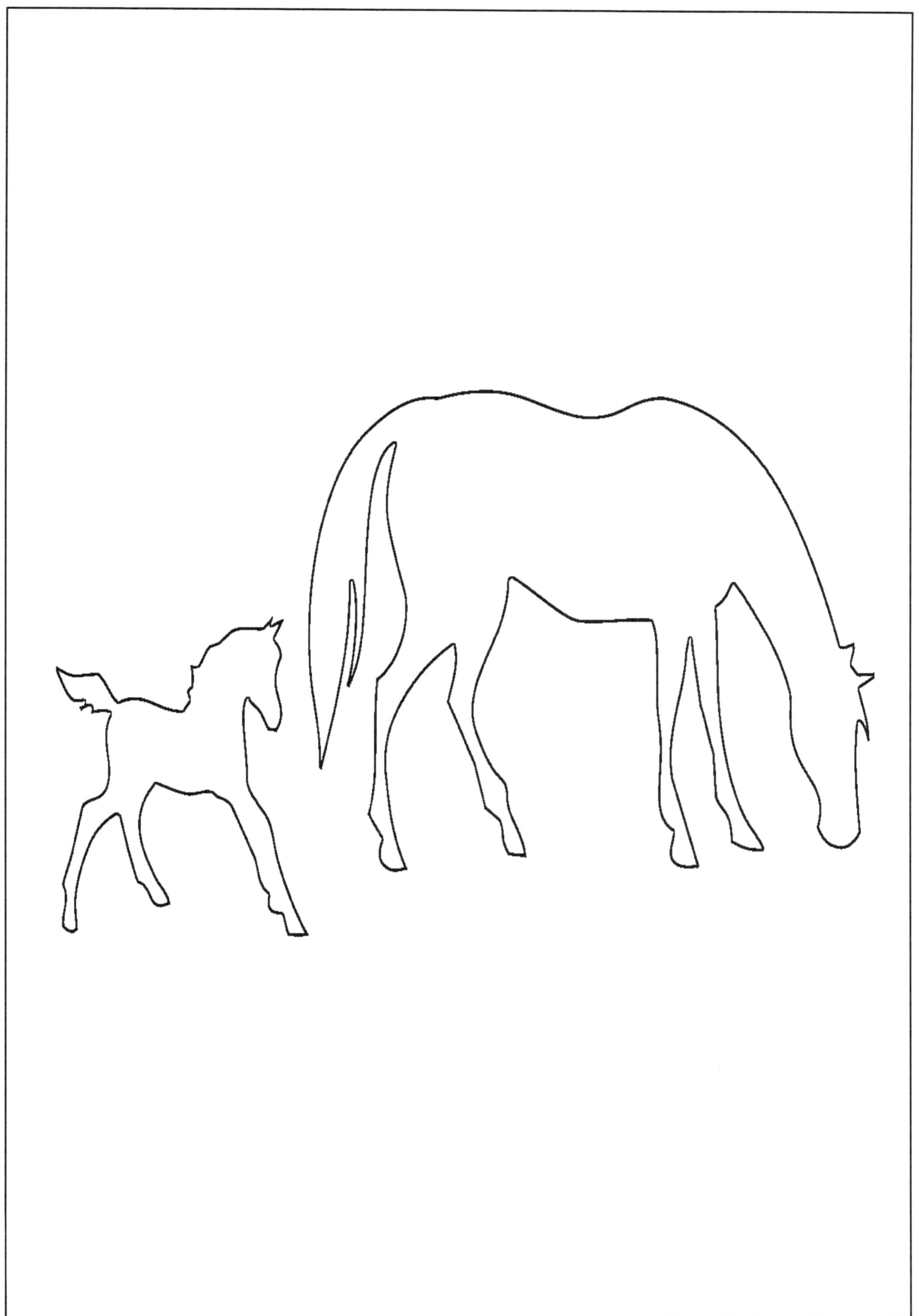

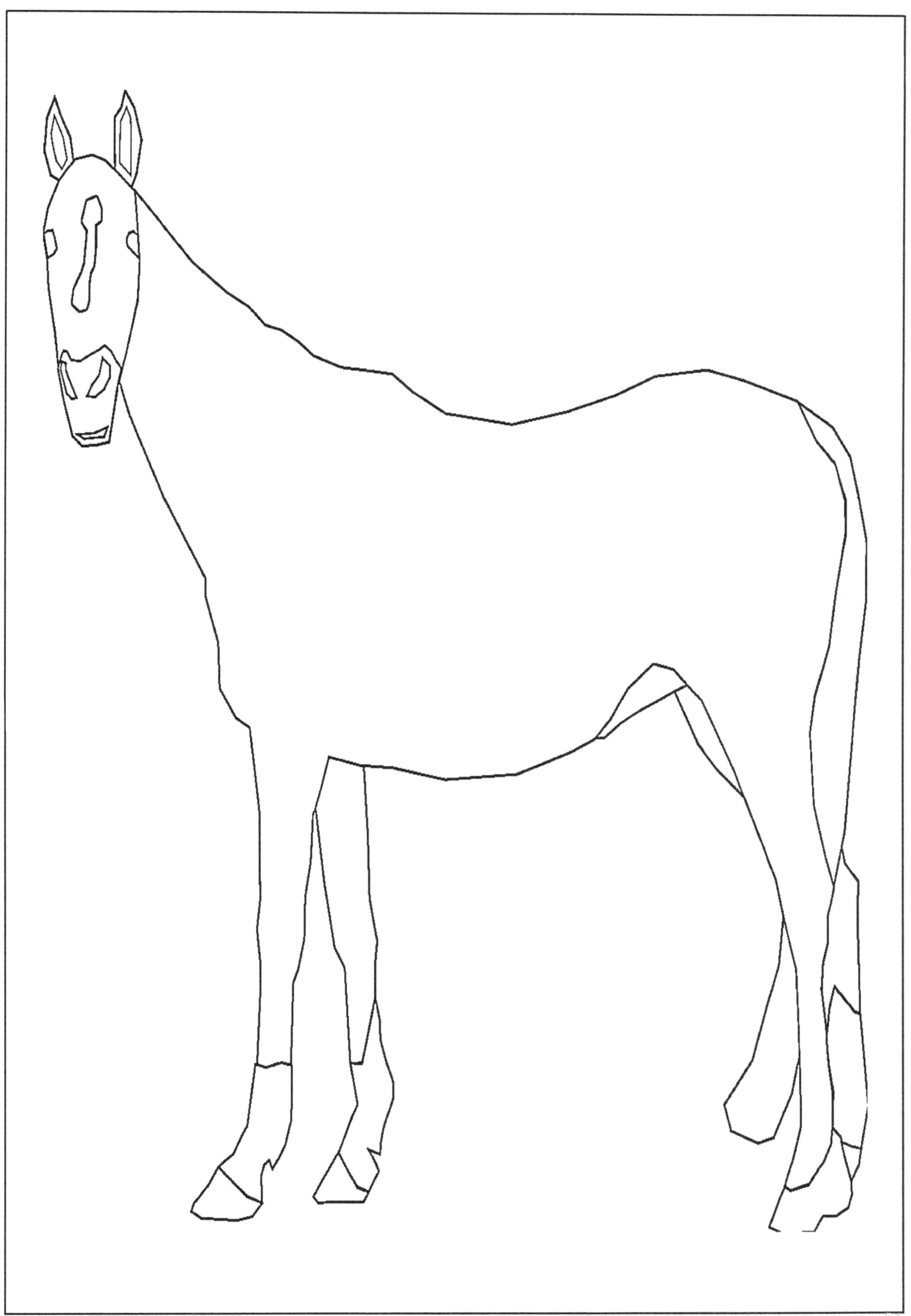

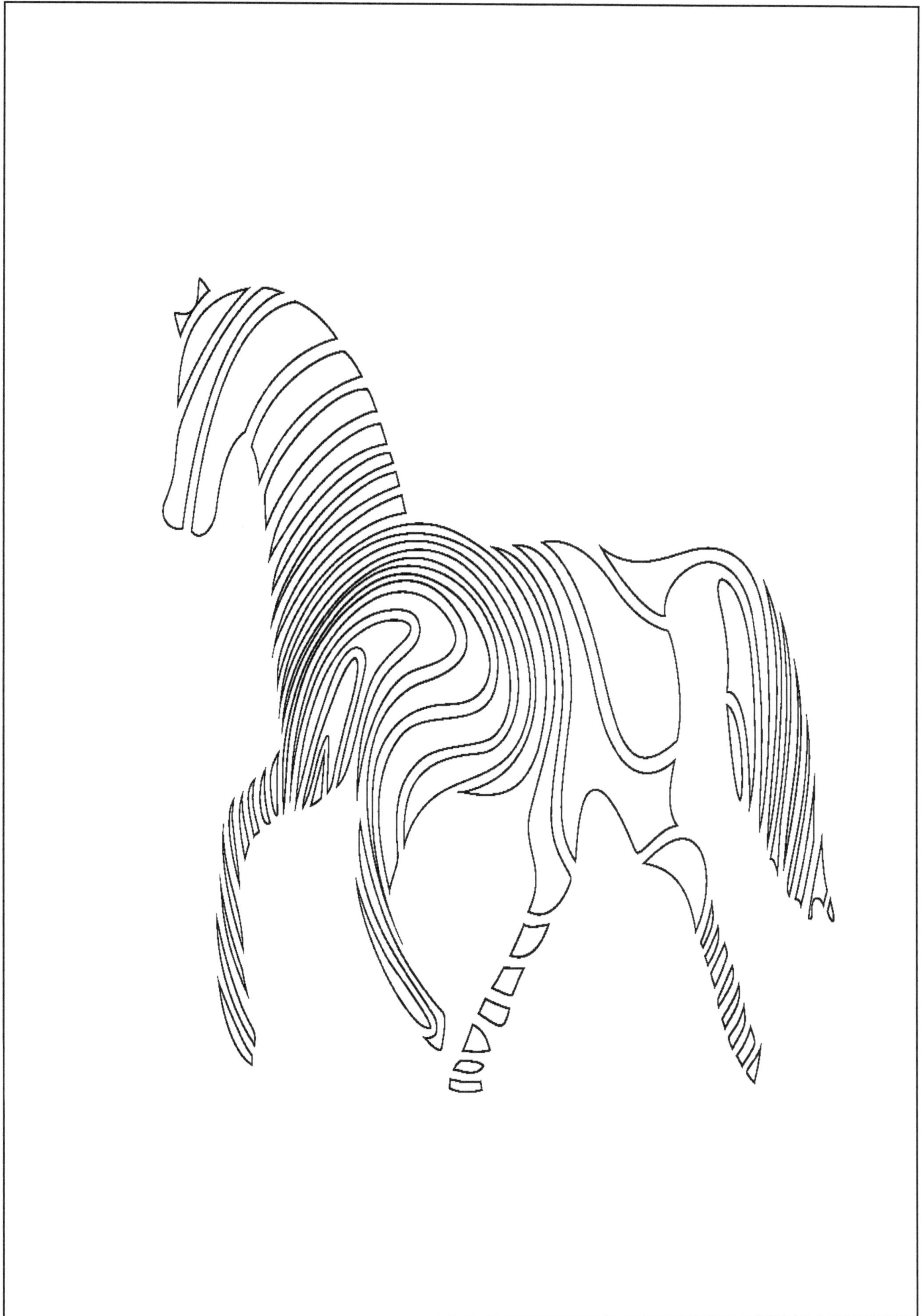

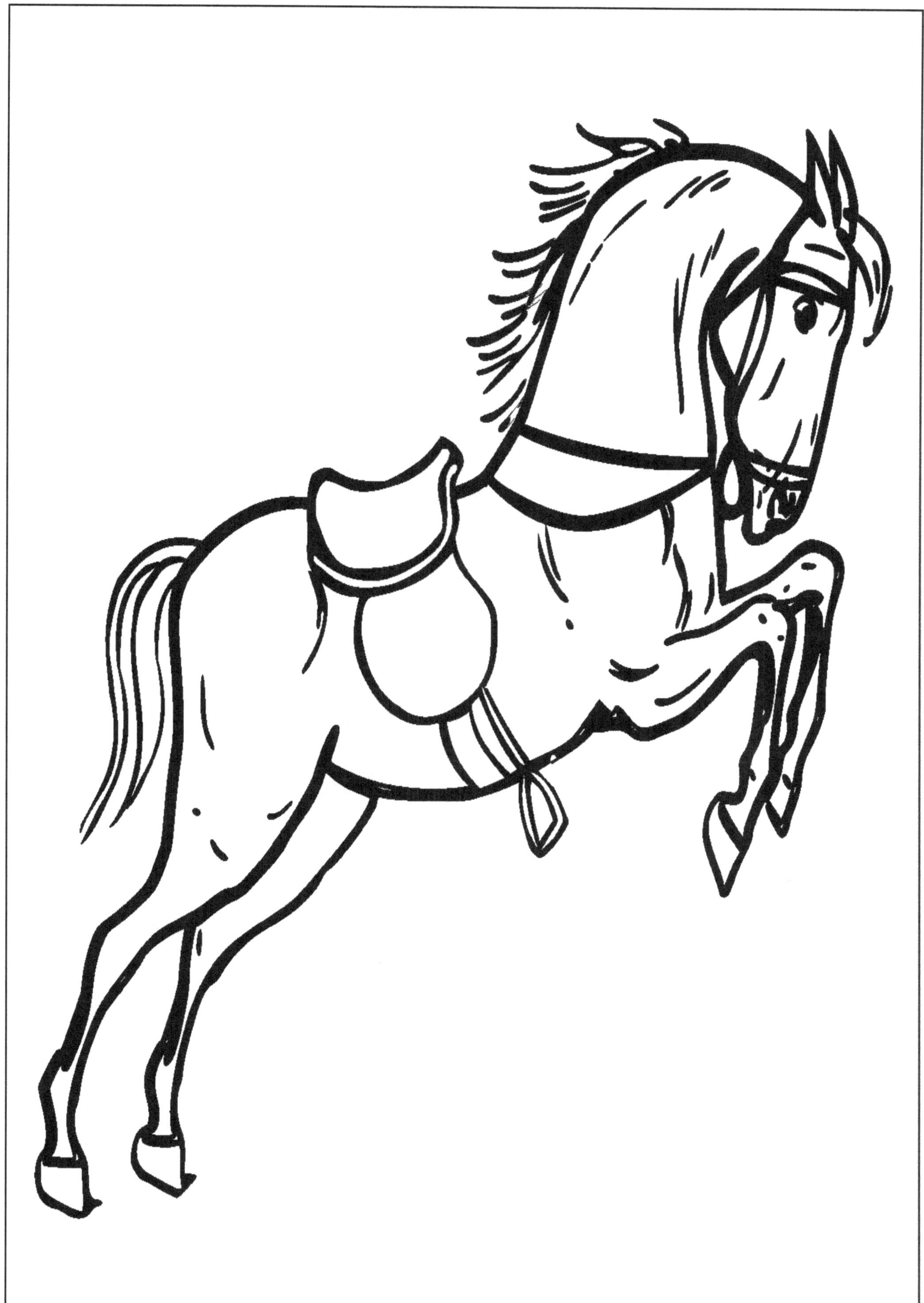